THE HEART CREMATES ITSELF

'The Heart Cremates Itself:
A Poetry Chapbook'
Copyright © Tadhg Culley 2022.
Cover Image by Isabella Mariana at Pexels

Contact the author at:
undotheheartbreak@gmail.com

ISBN: 9798840886113

Copyright Notice: All rights reserved. Without limiting the rights under copyright reserved above, no part of this publication may be reproduced, stored in or introduced into a retrieval system, or transmitted, in any form, or by any means (electronic, mechanical, photocopying, recording, or otherwise) without the prior written permission of the copyright owner of this book, except for brief quotations embodied in critical reviews and certain other non-commercial uses permitted by copyright law.

TADHG CULLEY

'The Heart Cremates Itself'

I remember their bedrooms,
Their music playlists,
As if I went collecting,
Song recommendations.

It was by far the best,
When conversations flowed,
When connections ran deep,
When dreams were shared.

But after I had left,
As their perfume faded,
A part of their souls,
Recommended songs…

Now, many years later,
When I hear such music,
My heart cremates itself,
Into burnt passion's ashes.

THE HEART CREMATES ITSELF

'The Heart Is A Stopwatch'

The seconds melt into minutes,
The minutes melt into hours,
The hours melt into days,
The days melt into weeks,
The weeks melt into months,
The months melt into years,
The years melt into decades,
And life drifts by like that...

But the heart has a stopwatch;
Split-second love is stirred,
Time stands still...
(Such feelings immortalized).

Your life rolls on and on,
As you get *so* much older,
While "undying love" dies,
The heart never forgets...

(To top it all off,
My time's forever frozen,
I think my stopwatch,
Broke long ago...)

Perhaps I need repairing.

TADHG CULLEY

'The Heart's Battlefield'

My heart has seen too many wars and battles,

How many times can it be attracted?
How many times can it be wooed?
How many times can it be enamoured?
How many times can it be seduced?
How many times can it be romanced?
How many times can it be loved?

I wonder, will I raise my sword once more?
As my shining steed charges into war,
With hundreds o' battlefields in hindsight,
Perhaps we only have a few fights left!
My face won't glow like a naïve man,
My eyes won't twinkle as they did before...

It still pumps blood around my battlements,
But my heart can't love like it did before.

THE HEART CREMATES ITSELF

'At Croxden Abbey'

I wandered around ruins at Croxden,
Whose abbey walls still stand so tall...
Walking my miniature dachshund,
Mind roaming through past centuries,
Dreaming of far better times,
Viewing open graves and tombs,
Whose lids have long-since cracked off,
Marvelling at fine archways,
In awe of skilled stonemasonry.
Remaining in 21st Century,
I re-entered the 12th Century.
Until a little girl arrived,
Who'd lurked behind me softly,
I heard the gentle pitter-patter,
Of timid, curious footsteps.
She took me out of time travel,
Lifted me out of trance,
Since she wished to stroke my pooch...
But my little dog got scared,
I laughed, "Don't worry, he's just so much,
Smaller than you are, my dear,
If I was him, I'd be scared too".
Then this intrigued little girl,
Who stood perhaps four-foot-tall,
Said with absolute certainty,
"Oh, I know that already..."
She glanced so far up at me,
Squinting in the sunlight,
(Since I stand at 6'3"),
And I was put in place by *her!*
Returning her inquisitive gaze,
Back to my gorgeous daxie,
She was pensively pondering,

TADHG CULLEY

The sight of my nervous hound,
Then she said this perfect sentence,
Which finds me penning this poem:
"He wants to get to know new people,
But he's not so sure any more, is he?".
I inwardly chuckled at that,
And at this precocious lass,
Then off she ran to play,
To continue with her day!
Trampling the grass banks,
Leaping from the ruin's rocks,
Getting grass-stains on holed socks,
No doubt making observations,
At one-hundred miles-an-hour,
On I wandered, around,
What was left of Croxden Abbey,
Viewing rock and ruin,
And ghost-like blurry movement,
Of fascinated little girl,
Whose soul, alight, inspired,
Transmitted light into my being.
I grew transfixed by the idea,
Of who she might one day become,
(Since she was already a writer,
By the age of ten and one!).
Such pleasant observation,
Aimed at my little dog:
"He wants to get to know new people,
But he's not so sure any more, is he?".
I realized her simple statement,
Profoundly applied to me!
I basked in the shadow,
Of this Cistercian abbey,
Where I also found myself to be,
A ruin.

THE HEART CREMATES ITSELF

'At Buildwas Abbey'

While walking my dog,
At Buildwas Abbey,
Admiring stone archways,
That still stand to this day,
I discovered an artist,
Who worked with charcoal,
Painting with her fingertips,
Beneath the ancient Sun,
Recapturing lost grandeur,
As if stolen beauty could still be won,
Despite being lost to time,
Enduring the cost of existence,
For lasting through the centuries.

We spoke sweet nothings,
Of her art and mine,
Of how we are outlasted,
By creations that we build,
These stone walls,
Her canvas scratchings,
My paper scrawlings,
While clouds passed over us,
As if they were our lives,
And gentle breeze brushed by,
Like cotton-thread of our time here,
Something started carrying our souls,
Across the centuries…

TADHG CULLEY

'It's All Coming Together, (It's All Falling Apart)'

It's all coming together,
(It's all falling apart),
Like passing clouds that form,
Full shapes, formerly halved.

When you're thinking deeply,
Thoughts flow purest tides,
Words can be aligned,
With songs heard on device.

This sweetest mystery,
Of synchronicity,
Blessed my fruitful years,
Grown out of perished tears.

But like recurring numbers,
777, 333,
I find some words o'erlap,
With serendipity.

Say, if I think of "Beauty",
I'd hear it in a song,
Split-second I wrote it down,
Which tells me, *all is found*.

Proves things are flowing well,
I'm finally aligned,
As if I am on track,
To capture Destiny.

THE HEART CREMATES ITSELF

'Nightmare Tomb'

I have this repeating dream,
Where I am in a tomb,
Of ancient origin.
A mix of Rome and Greece,
With a hint of Egypt,
Though of an undiscovered,
Wyrd civilization.
It's deep underground,
Oh, so, so far down…
You have to crawl on belly,
Where time-lost sands are mixed,
With lost-soul human ashes.
Archaeologically unfound.
Here or there, a relic,
Of glass-like instrument,
Made o' onyx or obsidian,
Shaped into urns or knives,
Steals all lives that delve there.
I know that my unwanted,
Nightly nightmare sojourns,
Are unwelcome too…
I am a trespassing visitant,
Who has not paid their admission,

Yet

I have this repeating dream,
Where I am in a tomb,
Of ancient origin.

I wonder if it's being prepared,
For me.

TADHG CULLEY

'That Gaze'

Though that gaze contains all ancient mysteries,
Of countless, untold, sacred histories,
Of bones in the ever-hungry dirt,
Of dried blood that floods the thirsty Earth,
Of whispers from forgotten, broken tombs,
Of screeches from torn-open, bleeding wombs,
Of speeches from each human tongue that lied,
Of teachings from each human being that died,
Of lessons from each human soul that fried,
Though that gaze controls and sells the World…

Do not gaze back into that lidless eye!

THE HEART CREMATES ITSELF

'Stories Whispered'

There are some stories that are required,
To be yelled from a fiery mountain,
There are some others that must be told,
While lying beneath a frozen throne,
This one that I dare not relay,
Is one that must be *whispered*,
On blackest midnight...
To pen such words in ink,
Beneath shadowy candlelight,
Is far too bold a task,
And yet I must, *I must*;
But if these words e'er saw the light of day,
Hell on Earth is surely sent your way.

This one that I dare not relay,
Is one that must be *whispered*.

The faintest sound is given to such task,
Since you must now dare to unmask,
All that is muttered into deaf ears,

Take it your grave.

Listen closely...
Are you willing?
(No, I thought as much).
So close your ears and eyes and mouth and mind.

Never listen to a story,
Whispered.
Never listen to a whisper,
Sold.

TADHG CULLEY

'These Endless Questions'

What's for dinner tonight?
What's the time right now?
What are you up to this weekend?
How's your night going?
How's your day been?
So have you got the time or not?
What's the weather like over there?
What are you doing at this very moment?
What's the date today?
Have you checked your emails?
Did you get that text?
Was there any post today?
Is the parcel on its way?
Did you pay the bills?
Have you done the washing up?
Are the plates put away?
Did you leave the oven on?
Did you lock the door?
Did you take the rubbish out?
Did you mow the lawn?
So have you put the bins out or not?
Have you done the laundry?
Did you get the groceries?
Did you sleep at all?
When did you go to bed?
What time did you get up?
(So when can I come over???)
All these questions,
And so many more,
Waste my time and yours...
Just tell me,
What lies inside your soul?
(...That is all I really need to know).

THE HEART CREMATES ITSELF

'My Heart's Retirement'

My heart seeks out retirement,
Before a life of work,
At 32, from too much suffering,
My heart deals out refinement.

To find a foreign mirage-land,
Made of naught but fantasy,
Where hummingbirds whizz by,
Existing in the fiction of my mind.

My heart seeks out retirement,
Before retirement age,
A life of work still yet to come,
Despite so many loves lost.

My heart seeks out retirement,
Unable to afford the cost,
Incapable of beating freely,
It simply has forgotten how…

My heart seeks out retirement,
So it has the time, and peace enough,

To learn how to die.

TADHG CULLEY

'Summer's Bounty'

As trees reach up high for the skies,
As flowers dare to lift their heads,
As everything on Planet Earth,
Stretches for the molten Sun.

Dreaming of a Summer's bounty,
Remembering Springs aplenty.

It is too far, and far too easy,
To fall into 'eternal love',
Every time, each new season,
Sensing Summertime.

Fall in love,
In the dead of Winter,
While everything around you perishes,
And then I might believe you...

I tend to fall in love at Autumn's curse,
With those icy winds ne'er relenting,
While the trees seem so skeletal,
Poking branches, pointing bone-like, at:

What by Wintertime,
My love becomes...

THE HEART CREMATES ITSELF

'Ships Of Stone Seen In The Sky'

The clouds were ships that sailed o'erhead,
Lying on our backs, our eyes found skies,
With her hand upon my beating chest,
She gazed into my gaze and then she asked:

"What shall we talk about on this fine day?",
I said, "Spotting shapes in clouds is too cliché...,
So spot some shapes within my eyes instead",
She giggled, brushing her hand down my ribs.

With love in mind, she soon drew back in terror,
She could've said, "I saw gravestones in there",
Instead, she lied, changing conversation,
(Switching to the topic writers hate).

She spoke of clouds, "I see a ship! Do you?",
I blinked and took her hand from off my crotch,
Replying, "You should tell me what you've seen,
While deeply eye-gazing into my soul".

I said, "Besides, I see no ships but stones",
Her eyes replied to mine wordlessly,
Returning to our backs, parting touch,
To soak up Grecian azure up above.

I felt bad for what I'd said. She'd not wished,
To impart what she'd seen within my pupils,
Apologizing, *turning, rolling, kissing,*
She dared ask, "So whose death had you seen?".

TADHG CULLEY

"Was it mine or yours?". I said, "...Neither".
She questioned, "So whose gravestone did I see?".
"You witnessed the graveyard of my heart,
Though still alive, you glimpsed all my lost loves".

But sharing such a harsh truth as that,
Knowing I'd ne'er love the way I did,
We never spoke again of deep eye-gazing,
If asked again, I'll stick to cloud clichés...

THE HEART CREMATES ITSELF

'Art Straight From The Heart'

Don't o'er-intellectualize it,
I'll do my best to keep this "simply put",
This artist's craft is oft performed within,
What seems to be mysterious States of Flow.
To strange points where we can get all poetic,
And claim to say things like "It flowed straight through me",
"I don't e'en know where it could've come from",
My memory is so bad that I can read,
Something that I'd written long ago,
Forgetting I'd e'en been the one to write it,
(Which is often pleasantly surprising),
Because, by now, I've written quite a lot!
Sticking to original intention,
Of keeping this short poem "simply put",
I shall now sum this feeling up for you:

In States of Flow, access your subconscious,
Simply get the fuck out your own way!
Do that, bring true Art straight from the Heart,
...Don't o'er-intellectualize it.

TADHG CULLEY

'The Heart Holds Your Family Tree'

To think that through my beating heart,
Flows my Family Tree,
Is such a comforting notion to me,
Blood flowing free like fine red wine,
Of Pinot Noir variety,
(Which just so happens to be,
My favourite indulgence),
As I crack open this rare bottle,
To celebrate career so far,
I feel my heart pouring out,
My ancestry.

I have known grief far too many times,
I have lost too many loved ones,
I need only place my warmest hand,
Upon my beating ribcage,
To reconnect with lifeforce,
That sustains me,
That birthed me,
That carried me,
'Cross fierce oceans,
And hellish tides,
Which still protects me to this very day.

When I become someone to remember,
To mourn and miss, cry over, maybe grieve,
Do not worry, my blood shall only pour,
From another sought-after bottle,

Into yours.

THE HEART CREMATES ITSELF

'Capture This Exuberance'

Sometimes I wish that every soul on Earth,
Could feel to the depths that I do,
While at times my days are living Hell,
While at others I drift through Purgatory,
Some lucky days I'm lifted up to Heaven,
Where I soar with stars in dolphin-flight,
I see the World exactly how it is,
Where I behold the Majesty of Art,
While plucking strings within the Planet's Heart,
I can feel so deeply I become,
Jealous of myself within this state.

If I could only bottle this sensation,
I'd be the richest man on Planet Earth.
Yet I have never chased such finest riches,
(Let's be real, I'm a poet after all)
However, this rich pauper safely says,
The closest that I've e'er managed to come,
Capturing exuberant sensation,
Is found within this eternal poem.

TADHG CULLEY

'Play Jester'

I am smart and wise enough to know,
That I am just a fool and nothing more,
That's enough responsibility, thanks,
In fact, (actually, come to think of it),
I may well have to shirk this serious duty...

Play at being Jester, with no commitment,
To the role, after all, the low pay sucks!
Anyway, far too few laugh at my jokes!
Why play the Fool when you can fail at that?

Now, I wonder, what must I,
Be foolish at next?

THE HEART CREMATES ITSELF

'Our Endless Error'

We are devils writing about angels,
Mere mortals dreaming of the heavens,
Why does allocated time-and-place,
Not suffice for humankind?

The daily bounty. The murky seas.
The azure skies. The raven clouds.
The birds that fly. The dogs that bark.
The Sun that coats our tanning bark.

The nightly duty. The stars. The Moon.
The mysteries of this Universe.
Why is all that life can offer,
Not enough for humankind?

Why must we glance at the Unseen?
Why must we hark at the Unheard?
Why must we sense the great Unknown?
When our endless error is being human...

TADHG CULLEY

'Do Not Commit To Paper'

I can't record what I want to write,
On my phone or on my laptop,
Call me paranoid,
(This is just a poem after all...)

But the Planet's Burning!
While the World's Drowning!

This poem must be burned at sea,
To honour modern travesty,
Such stories I am hearing,
(Those not involving me,
But strictly told to me),
Are (almost) more than I can bear.

(If I wasn't trained for this,
From birth and throughout life,
I might not manage the hearing of 'em).
Military Veterans have bent my ear,
Some were even Court-Marshalled,
Before wagging their chins at me.

I don't know who to believe any more,
But knowing what little I know,
Fucking hell, they have stories to tell,
Which might well sell a book or two...

Which often makes me wonder,
What did Hunter S. Thompson,
Or Charles Bukowski,
Not commit to paper?
Since state secrets can get you killed,
This is the life-or-death business,

THE HEART CREMATES ITSELF

The pen far mightier than the horde,
Or the sword they also wield,
What you write in this short life,
Might bring about a hasty death.

Hence why I won't rush to record,
Such stories spun that twist my ear,
Be careful what you write about,
Especially when these twisting tales,
Are not your own...

Since they were not brave enough,
To write them down themselves.

Some things spoken of while drunk,
Should not be committed to paper,
Yet this is one tool of our trade,
In this modern day and age,
It is one source of our craft,
Yet still I listen in bars, pubs and clubs.

Be careful of what you commit to paper,
Especially when it comes from someone else...

TADHG CULLEY

'Six Languages'

She fucked me in six languages,
Three I understood,
Two I did not,
(One I'm sure she made up...)

'Til all that was between us,
Was a stream of wordless liquid,
New language existed,
Upon and within,
Our sacred bodies.
Glistening.

In pools of lust,
In caves of love,
In caverns of loss.

Until it all,
Got wiped up.

THE HEART CREMATES ITSELF

'Inseparably Linked'

Sex and Death are inseparably linked,
Both seem to come from a similar void,
The Womb is a kiln-like Tomb,
The Tomb is an urn-like Womb.
Both harvest ecstasy,
With blinding pleasure,
To the point that,
Nothing else can be known,
But Sex and Death.

One gives life,
The other takes it.
One breeds life,
The other fakes it.
One needs life,
The other makes it.

Each transmutes it,
Into something else,
To somewhere else,
From some place else.

The Womb is a kiln-like Tomb,
The Tomb is an urn-like Womb.

Sex and Death are inseparably linked,
Both seem to come from a similar feud,

Yet neither create light,
Only New Life...

TADHG CULLEY

'The Pyre, My Pyre'

The pyre my body burns on,
Is not made out of wood,
But torn-out, shredded papers,
From my life's work in books.

Of countless conversations,
With ex-cons and drugged-drunks,
Of endless wanderings,
On cobbled streets of blood.

Of ceaseless manias,
'Neath Islay whisky full-moons,
Of red wine-bottle hearts,
From many more lost lovers.

The pyre my body burns on,
Is made of something else…
Filled condoms thrown in bins,
And tissues soaked in jizz.

Where many a vacant hanny-hour,
Replaced a drunken happy-hour,
To hang the head in pride-filled shame,
Instead of hanging neck in noose.

To stumble past the homeless,
To smile at star-eyed hookers,
To find a home where no-one lives,
Where wood might fuel a fire…

Fit for a hearth,
…But not my pyre.

THE HEART CREMATES ITSELF

'Wino'

This was a Spring-filled Summer,
Of heightened hay-fever,
Walking miles on marathons,
Through time-lost, ancient ruins,
With a bottle o' wine each night,
To keep our souls alight.
I doubt it's a coincidence,
That favourite '667',
From Monterey, California,
A finest Pinot Noir,
(While indulging in others),
A mix of cheap bottles,
And expensive splurges,
Each night, we sank more than one bottle,
Through this Spring-filled Summer,
Since we had some time off work,
Which was a treat as rare as the wine,
Which we drank as if it was each other's blood…

To savour each night,
We savour each bottle,
To savour our lives.

So, here's to "the good life"!,
Clink with me, "Bonae Vitae!"
Savouring golden-time,
'Til Autumn's ice-Winter,
By then I'll quit being Wino,
Which is a sign I must,

Get sober and go dry,
Before blood runs awry.

TADHG CULLEY

'Sometimes... Until...'

Sometimes there's no greater feeling than:

Clean bedsheets,
A full fridge,
An uncorked bottle,
A wallet with cash stashed,
A pocket with coins hidden,
A pregnant conversation,
An orgasm's eruption.
Where all the problems in your life,
And all the chaos of the world,
Can wait. *Until...*
The bedsheets need changing,
The fridge needs restocking,
The bottle needs refilling,
The money needs earning,
The conversation's lacking,
The game needs dining,
Where all the problems in your life,
And all the chaos in the world,
Can't wait. *Until...*
There are clean bedsheets,
A full fridge,
An uncorked bottle,
A wallet with cash stashed,
A pocket with coins hidden,
A pregnant conversation,
An orgasm's eruption.
Where all the problems in your life,
And all the chaos of the world,
Can wait.

...Until...

THE HEART CREMATES ITSELF

'Shadows And Shades Of Love'

The memories faded,
The photos burned,
The letters torn-up,
The cards discarded,
The notes destroyed,
The gifts donated,
Their faces forgotten,
Their songs misremembered,
Their lyrics misquoted,
Their names mispronounced,
Their bodies long-lost,
Their thoughts outdated,
Their lust satiated.

With romance undone,
And grief spent,
Now heartbreak has healed.

I linger on,
To live on,
And love again,

For what?

TADHG CULLEY

'Marshmallow Hearts'

Let's melt marshmallows,
Over the open campfire,
That is my charred heart.

Let's toast some s'mores,
Over the licking flames,
Of my spent soul.

Before the hazy smoke,
Can burn our eyes to blindness,
Let's dissolve our romance.

Let's simply leave,
Our midnight snacks,
For someone else.

Evaporate with me,
Into the starlight-pact.

THE HEART CREMATES ITSELF

'Critics At Reception'

Why worry about critical reception?
For that to take place, your work must be read,
Since that may not happen 'til after you're dead,
Why let critical opinion burrow into your head?

Who cares what the nation thinks? Or internationally?
That is mere extension of *what others think*,
And they all tell you to ignore that, don't they?
Ironically, they've trained us not to care what they say.

My work is written for myself or meant in jest,
(To hide the fact that some speak truths of my soul),
Let critics think the best of my work was the price,
To pay for the burden of bringing forth my worst.

In fact, reverse that sentiment, my worst,
Is the price you pay to get the best off my chest,
The world has gone to shit! Which makes it fertile ground,
To bring about a better time, like those that have long passed.

Call my follies "manure" and life can grow from them,
After all, I've not yet been blessed with children,
To pass such lessons on, to take my steaming baton;
Remember, growth is just another name for decay.

TADHG CULLEY

'The Vampire's Bite'

If given the right to immortal life,
On Planet Earth, here and now,
I would not take it. My interests,
Do not concern what is to come,
But what has gone. All that has been,
Lost to ancient sands of time…

If the vampire's bite arrived,
In 2022AD, I'd fly into the Sun.
But ask me in 2022BC,
And I'd desire to live forever.
To bare witness to the cultures,
That were born and have since perished.

To understand Egypt. To marvel at Rome.
To breathe in Greece. To unfold Neolithic.
To see standing stones rise.
To feel dolmens form.
To know stone age burial rites,
To understand the night.

Lost mysteries of Druidry,
Gods. Goddesses. Living Pantheons.
Don't let vampire's bite strike this year,
But take me back to a time where,
Life was worth living, with knowledge given;

If bitten in 2022BC,
I'd seek sunlight by 2022AD.

THE HEART CREMATES ITSELF

'That Is All'

Everybody's human,
That is all...
Everybody thinks,
Of selling their soul,
Everybody needs,
The same ole thing,
Everybody wants,
Everything,
Everybody feels,
Past sell-by-date,
Everybody sees,
Their own suffering,
Everybody loves,
A made-up scene,
Everybody dreams,
Their grass more green,
Everybody hopes,
For one more chance,
Everybody copes,
With chosen poison,
Everybody falls,
To rock bottom,
Everybody soars,
To heights forgotten.

Everybody lies,
To escape their lives,
Everybody lives,
To one day die.

TADHG CULLEY

'Drown By Wine'

My brain floats in wine,
When thoughts of mine sail her way,
Soul spins and swoons,
Despite my heavy frame,
Heart pumps out molten iron,
To swell surging chest,
To harden each region,
Of mortal design.

When she leans to press,
Her plump lips against mine,
I feel so alive,
That I might die.

THE HEART CREMATES ITSELF

'Beneath His Nose'

He wore an ever-present look,
Upon his leather-wrinkled face,
As if tucked beneath his nose,
Always lingered white dog shit.

His expression only occurred,
After meeting me…
Learning how I stole her heart,
From his basement-birdcage.

TADHG CULLEY

'Summer BBQ'

Poke the glowing embers,
Beneath this BBQ,
As the Sun goes down,
These flames shall follow suit.

With shrimps on the barby,
Screaming searing silence,
Our eyes met, as they grilled,
And her sharpened blow-poke,

In that scalding heat,
Found my ashen heart.

THE HEART CREMATES ITSELF

'Socks & Sandals'

She wore sweaty socks and sandals,
But somehow made it fashionable,
While she spoke honest trifles,
She found hidden poetic kernels.

She rarely wore bold make-up,
Bur ne'er e'er ceased to glow,
Her hair, a tangled, messy bee-hive,
Contained secrets of the Universe.

In her smelly socks and sandals,
She declared herself a Queen,
As if her regal, unique scent,
Taught me how that must be true.

Since no-one could ever deny,
The stream of her forgotten bloodline.

TADHG CULLEY

'Mercenary Mechanic'

Life is one long road,
Littered with potholes,
With no lay-bys for repair,
Life is an empty gas tank,
With no petrol station near,
Life is a chipped windscreen,
That spreads to crack and shatter,
Life is a flapping flat tyre,
With no spare in the boot,
Life is a bird-shit splattered screen,
With no screen wash, with broken wipers,
Life is a gearbox stuck in reverse,
That only knows how to stall,
Life is a blocked exhaust pipe,
Hoping to choke us all.

THE HEART CREMATES ITSELF

'Past/Present/Passed'

We can't escape our Past,
It is always present,
In the Present,
As a present,
In our blood,
In our people,
In our land,
History chases us,
From the ancient,
Into the modern,
Our brains cannot fathom,
Frantic development,
Never-ending,
Never-ceasing,
Yet our hearts still know,
We are hunter-gatherers,
In robotic age,
Spitting stories around,
Neon campfires…

Dare to stare me in the eye,
And if you have the strength,
To maintain my gaze,
To earn the right,
To survive that rite,
You just might,
Catch a glance,
Or even a spark,
Of my living ancestry,
Entangled with yours,

Burning while frozen.

TADHG CULLEY

'Be Careful'

Be careful of the poems that you write,
I was penning Death and then I died,
Somehow brought back into this life,
While my fevered brain endured a trial.

I underwent delirium tremens,
To put me with the likes of E. A. Poe,
Hallucinating demons, seeing insects,
As I battled insomnia's stake.

I heard splintered songs on endless repeat,
With broken sentences from passersby,
Everything was an accusation,
The voice inside my mind burnt me alive.

A paramedic, a doctor and a nurse,
All told me how this could've proven fatal,
A hellish week was neither hit nor missed,
I was planning how to meet my Maker.

Until I sit here, able to pen poesy,
Understanding that I must scribe warning,
Be careful of the poems that you write,
From now, I hope, mine only speak of life.

THE HEART CREMATES ITSELF

<ins>Other Written Works by Tadhg Culley</ins>

Novellas – Available on Amazon

'Secrets Hidden In The Walls (A Collection Of 8 Novellas)
'Secrets Trapped In The Attic' (A Collection Of 4 Novellas)
'Secrets Locked In The Basement' (A Collection Of 4 Novellas)
'The Poet And The Prostitute'
'The Holler Screams'
'Gridlock Deadlock'
'Urban Expiration'
'Coming Soon To Cinemas Near You'
'Mirror's Eye Motel'
'Soul Tax'
'Womb Tomb'
'The Cold Walls Of A Warm Heart' (A Novelette)

Short Story Collection – Available on Amazon
'Secrets Buried In The Woods'

Memoir – Available on Amazon
'Paperback Silverback'

Poetry Books – Available on Amazon
'The Complete Poetical Works Of Tadhg Culley' (Volume of 288 poems)
'Undo the Heartbreak' (Anthology of 150 poems)
'Unsung Lyricality' (Anthology of 68 poems)
'Relive the Romance' (Chapbook of 34 poems)
'Red Glows Only Lovers Know' (1 long poem)
'Melancholic Moments' (Chapbook of 21 poems)
'Shards Of A Ceramic Soul' (Chapbook of 15 poems)
'True Love Might (Not) Exist' (Chapbook of 7 poems)
'Love Glutton' (Anthology of 75 poems)
'Songs That Shake My Soul' (Collection of 45 poems)
'The Snake, The Scorpion, The Sage' (Book of 38 poems)
'The Written Word' (Book of 36 poems)

About the Author

Tadhg Culley is a Professional Screenwriter, Published Author and Poet from the UK. He has written over five-hundred poems, nineteen audiobooks, ten feature film screenplays, eight TV series scripts, eight novellas, three guidebooks, one memoir, one novelette, one collection of short stories, and many other short-form works, delving into short films, documentaries, theatre, animation and games. He is a BAFTA Scholar and graduate of both the National Film & TV School (NFTS) & the University of Creative Arts (UCA).

Printed in Great Britain
by Amazon